Can Jesus Go to School with Me Every Day?

Dr. Mary Rice-Crenshaw

Illustrated by Ashfand Yar Ashraf

WestBow Press books may be ordered through booksellers or by contacting:

WestBow Press
A Division of Thomas Nelson & Zondervan
1663 Liberty Drive
Bloomington, IN 47403
www.westbowpress.com
844-714-3454

Interior Image Credit: Ashfand Yar Ashraf

Scripture quotations taken from The Holy Bible, New International Version® NIV® Copyright © 1973 1978 1984 2011 by Biblica, Inc. TM. Used by permission. All rights reserved worldwide.

ISBN: 978-1-6642-4049-0 (sc)
ISBN: 978-1-6642-4050-6 (e)

Library of Congress Control Number: 2021914436

Print information available on the last page.

WestBow Press rev. date: 08/26/2021

WESTBOW
PRESS®
A DIVISION OF THOMAS NELSON
& ZONDERVAN

I acknowledge the guidance of the Holy Spirit.

Thank you to:

Courtney Singleton for your anointed creativity.

Mom and Dad for making Church and Sunday
School the norm in our family.

My husband for his unwavering support.

My spiritual support system local, state, and national.

My personal Westbow Press Publishing
Support Team. The process works.

Dr. Mary Rice-Crenshaw

Our children are faced with one crisis after another in our schools—school shootings, the COVID-19 pandemic, widespread social unrest, and the growing breakdown of the fiber of our families and our country. I often wonder how our children cope with having to go to school every day while dealing with so many pressures.

In 2005, I wrote a book for kids titled *Can Jesus Go to School with Me?* I wrote the book as I was preparing to deliver the back-to-school address to students enrolled in the district where I served as superintendent.

I was moved and encouraged to write yet another book, *Can Jesus Go to School with Me Every Day?* Our children are exposed to so much social media portraying unsafe schools that leave out many of the Christian values once taught to young people. We must assure children, parents, churches, and schools that Jesus is still everywhere, guiding, protecting, and loving little children. We can still sing with confidence that "Jesus loves the little children of the world." We can sing with hope in our hearts that "He's got the whole world in His hands." Most importantly, our children must be taught that Jesus cannot be legislated out of our schools because "He is everywhere."

A delightful uplifting read that offers our children hope. This book will inspire children of all ages. Dr. Crenshaw personalizes the interaction of the child with their emotions and stressors using a biblical perspective. Certainly, Jesus can go to school with each child every day.

Lesa Rice-Jackson, Ph.D.

For more than forty years, Dr. Mary Rice-Crenshaw has molded young minds. She has a passion for children and sees them as essential seeds in God's Kingdom. Dr. Rice-Crenshaw has a way of incorporating Christian values into the lives of our children with little effort.

This book alerts children and parents to remember that God is everywhere.

Dr. Rice-Crenshaw places God at the center of her teachings. Her values are vivid in her writings and everyday life. She tries to help everyone see God through their extraordinary lives.

Dr. Rice-Crenshaw is a dedicated nurturer. She has taught and mentored numerous students. This book expands our view that Jesus is everywhere.

Rev. Genetha Rice-Singleton, Master of Divinity, Emory University, Candler School of Theology

Dedicated to the little children of the world

He said to them, "Let the little children come to me, and do not hinder them, for the kingdom of God belongs to such as these. … And He took the children in His arms, placed his hands on them and blessed them" (Mark 10:14b, 16, NIV).

Can Jesus go to school with me every day?

Yes! He is everywhere.

He is on the bus.

He is in my car.

He is everywhere; no place is too far.

Can Jesus go to school with me every day?
Yes! He is everywhere.

He meets me at the school door
when my principal says hello.

He walks with me down the hall.

He is in the classroom as my teacher calls the classroom roll. "Present," I say.

Can Jesus go to school with me every day?
Yes! He is everywhere.

He is in the school cafeteria
while I am eating lunch.

He is with my friend and me in library while we read books.

Can Jesus go to school with me every day?
Yes! He is everywhere.

He is on the playground.

He is in my computer class.

He is even in my music class,
listening to me sing.

He's in my art class too!

Can Jesus go to school with me every day?
Yes! He is everywhere.

He is watching the children in every class.

He is with me when the bell rings to end the school day.

He is on the bus ride home to my house.

He is standing at my bus stop, watching as I get to my front door, and making sure I am safe and secure.

Can Jesus go to school with me every day?
Yes! He is everywhere.

Jesus is everywhere, with all the children and the teachers.

He is

   walking with us,

      talking to us,

         feeling how we feel,

            listening to us, and

               understanding us.

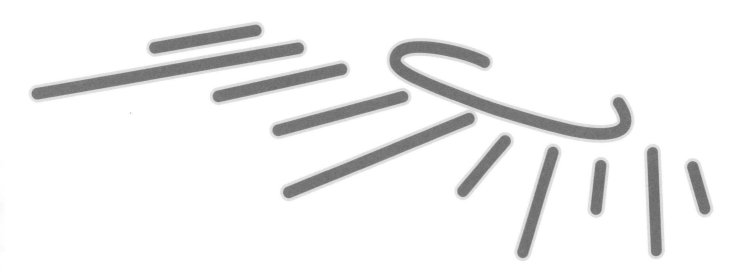

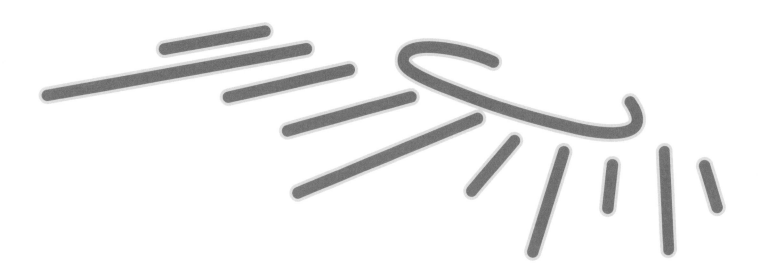

He is

caring for us,

protecting us,

teaching us, and

loving us.

Always!

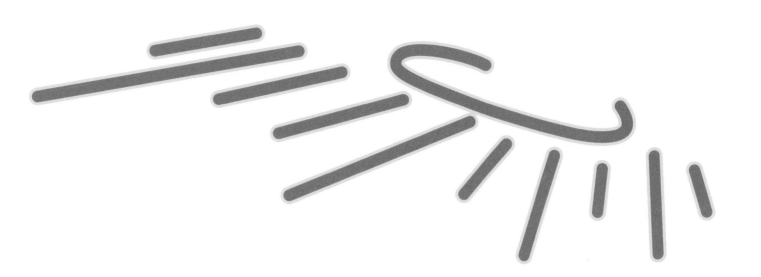

Can Jesus go to school with me every day?

Yes!

Jesus said,

"I am everywhere."